SMART INVESTMENT IN

CO₂ RECOVERY

SMART INVESTMENT IN CO_2 RECOVERY

Pulin Modi

Pendown Press

PREMIUM BUSINESS PUBLISHER

PENDOWN PRESS LLP

An ISO 9001 & ISO 14001 Certified Co.,

Regd. Office: 3767A, Kanhaiya Nagar,

Tri Nagar, Delhi-110035

Ph.: 8130886000, 9650072927

E-mail: info@pendownpress.com

Branch Office: 1A/2A, 20, Hari Sadan, Ansari Road,

Daryaganj, New Delhi-110002

Ph.: 011-45794768

Website: PendownPress.com

Edition: 2025

ISBN: 978-93-6338-451-4

Layout and Cover Designed by Pendown Graphics Team
Printed and Bound in India by Thomson Press India Ltd.

This book is dedicated to Mr. Farooque Dadabhoy, the visionary Chairman of Sicgil Group of Companies. With over 60 years of experience in India's CO_2 industry, his leadership and innovation have inspired many, including myself. I am proud to call him my role model and hope this book reflects the values of excellence and resilience he stands for.

Contents

Introduction — i

Preface — ii

Acknowledgements — iv

Why This Book? — v

Whom is This Book For? — vii

Value Addition for Readers — ix

1 — Capacity of CO2 Recovery Plant With Respect to Ethanol Plant Capacity — 1

2 — CO2 Plant Process Flow Diagram, Design, and Sizing of Equipment — 3

3 — Material of Construction of Equipment — 5

4 — Selection of CO2 Compressor & Selection of Ammonia Compressor — 7

5 — Design and Performance of Water-Cooled Heat Exchanger — 12

6	Why Ammonia as a Refrigerant?	14
7	Insulation of Low-Temperature Equipment	18
8	Easy Installation of SKID Mounted Plants	21
9	Instrumentation, Automation, Hazop Study of Plant	24
10	Desiccant Bed & Deodorizer Bed	27
11	Periodic Maintenance and Its Effect on Power Consumption	30
12	Training For Plant Operators & Engineers	33
	Fuel The Future	37

Introduction

Hello Readers,

I am Pulin Modi, a technocrat who graduated in Mechanical Engineering with a B.E. degree from L D College of Engineering, Ahmedabad. My professional journey in the Carbon Dioxide field started at SICGIL Industrial Gases Limited, where I started my career as a Works Manager.

With over 28 years of experience, I have developed expertise in various facets of the gas industry, particularly in process engineering and the design of Carbon Dioxide Recovery plants. This journey has propelled me to the esteemed position of Director - Safety & Technical at SICGIL Industrial Gases Limited.

In this book, I am delighted to share insights garnered from decades of hands-on experience and a deep understanding of CO2 recovery processes. Through a thorough exploration of key concepts, practical considerations, and industry best practices, my aim is to guide ethanol manufacturers with the knowledge about selection of CO2 recovery plants.

Preface

Have you ever wondered how a single decision could significantly impact the efficiency and sustainability of your ethanol plant? The choice to invest in a CO2 recovery plant is one such decision, and its implications are far-reaching. With the right information, this choice can lead to enhanced operational efficiency and substantial cost savings. Without it, you risk costly mistakes and operational setbacks.

This book is designed to address these very concerns. It provides a clear, practical guide for selecting a CO2 recovery plant-an investment that can transform your plant's performance and environmental footprint. Drawing on years of industry experience, I've crafted this guide to simplify the complexities of CO2 recovery technology and offer actionable insights that are both easy to understand and apply.

Throughout these pages, you'll find answers to essential questions: What should you look for in a CO2 recovery plant? How can you ensure that your investment delivers the desired results? What are the critical factors that will influence your decision?

By breaking down technical details into straightforward language, this book aims to empower you with the knowledge needed to make well-informed decisions. Whether you're an ethanol plant owner, a manager, or a consultant, this guide will help you navigate the selection process with confidence and clarity.

Thank you for allowing this book to be a part of your decision-making journey. I hope it serves as a valuable resource in achieving your plant's goals and optimizing your investment.

Warm regards,

Pulin Modi

Acknowledgements

As I represent SICGIL group, allow me to acquaint you with the legacy of SICGIL Group, a true pioneer in the business of Carbon Dioxide manufacturing and distribution. Since its inception in 1947, SICGIL has remained at the forefront of innovation, commanding an impressive market share of 25% in India's CO2 business landscape. With 77 years of experience, SICGIL has been fulfilling the needs of the industry, delivering an extensive range of products and services.

The SICGIL group's expertise provides CO2-related solutions, including tailor-made solutions for specific applications. This includes the design and manufacturing of CO2 recovery plants, specialized gas-related equipment, CO2 dosing systems for desalination plants and pH reduction systems, CO2 storage and transport tanks, the production and supply of ultra-high purity CO2 gas. SICGIL is also known for its commitment to quality and service in the supply of beverage-grade, weld-grade and various other grades of CO2. Additionally, SICGIL is the largest manufacturer of food-grade dry ice in India, serving the pharmaceutical industry for bulk drug manufacturing, ice cream industries, flight kitchens, and many other applications of dry ice.

Why This Book?

Let me share why I'm taking the time to write this book. You see, as part of SICGIL's CO2 gas business, we purchase Liquid Carbon Dioxide from various distilleries and ethanol plants that have their own CO2 recovery plants installed. Now, before we do business with them, we have a standard procedure where we audit their CO2 plants to ensure everything is in order. If we find any issues during the audit, we ask them to fix them before we proceed with any deals. Once everything checks out, we buy Liquid CO2 from them for our industrial applications.

During my visits to these plants, I have noticed some irregularities. Many of these CO2 plants are running in unsafe conditions; they are not very efficient, they are using excessive power, the conversion from raw CO2 gas to liquid CO2 ratio is very low, the quality of the produced liquid CO2 is not acceptable, the operators aren't properly trained, and the plants themselves are poorly maintained.

The above situation has disturbed me greatly. I discovered that one of the reasons for this situation is the installation of poorly designed CO2 plants. It made me realize that there is a lack of awareness and education among ethanol and alcohol producers about CO2 recovery plants. So, I've decided to take it upon myself to share what I've learned from my years in the gas industry. I want to give back to society by educating others about the selection guidelines for CO2 recovery plants. These selection guidelines will result in improved safety, efficiency, and effective operation once a CO2 recovery plant is installed.

Whom is This Book For?

This book is crafted for individuals who are at the forefront of decisions impacting ethanol plant's economical viability, particularly those contemplating the integration of CO2 recovery technology.

Specifically, it addresses:

➤ **Ethanol Plant Owners:** Those responsible for expanding or upgrading their facilities, seeking to understand the nuances of CO2 recovery plants and make choices that align with their operational goals.

➤ **Plant Managers and Engineers:** Professionals who will be directly involved in the selection, installation, and optimization of CO2 recovery systems, and who need practical, actionable insights to guide their decisions.

➤ **Technical Consultants and Advisors:** Experts providing recommendations to ethanol plants, who require a comprehensive understanding of CO2 recovery systems to offer well-informed guidance.

➤ **Procurement Specialists:** Individuals tasked with sourcing and evaluating high-capex equipment, and who need a thorough grasp of design criteria and operational considerations.

This book aims to empower these stakeholders with clear, technical knowledge, enabling them to confidently navigate the complexities of CO2 recovery plant selection and ensure their investments drive maximum value and efficiency.

Value Addition For Readers

➢ **Reduce Your Carbon Footprint:** Environmental Responsibility: Many customers aim to reduce their carbon footprint by capturing and repurposing CO2 emissions rather than releasing them into the atmosphere.

➢ **Convert Your Waste to Value:** One More Source of Income: Businesses may seek CO2 recovery solutions that are cost-effective, offering a good return on investment either through savings on emissions fees or by selling captured CO2 to various industries.

➢ **Follow the Law of the Land:** Regulatory Compliance: Some industries are subject to strict emissions regulations. Customers might require CO2 recovery plants to comply with these regulations and avoid penalties.

➢ **Have More Varieties in Your Product Basket:** Product Development: Companies in industries like food and beverage, pharmaceuticals, or agriculture may need CO2 for various processes. They seek CO2 recovery plants to obtain high-quality CO2 for use in their products.

➢ **Gain Knowledge About Key Parameters of CO2 Recovery Plants Before You Buy It:** Knowledge is Power. It will fulfill your expectation of reliable CO2 recovery plants to operate consistently, efficiently, and with minimal downtime, resulting in continuous production.

Capacity of CO2 Recovery Plant With Respect to Ethanol Plant Capacity

> *As a rule of thumb, for a 100 KLPD Ethanol manufacturing capacity, a 50 Tons per Day CO2 recovery plant can be installed.*

Theoretically, more raw CO2 is available from the distillery, but due to the batch process, the quantity and pressure of raw CO2 vary significantly. Consequently, CO2 plants installed with higher capacities may not perform optimally.

CO2 recovery plants are tailor-made designs. A crucial step in the design process is analyzing the purity of the raw CO2 and its impurities. This analysis report is essential as it ensures that the CO2 recovery plant is designed with sufficient additional capacity to handle any sudden increase in the impurities of individual components.

For example, Customer A and Customer B both need a CO2 recovery plant with a capacity of 100 Tons per day. However, the composition of impurities in their raw CO2 may differ. Let's assume Customer A's raw CO2 has higher levels of impurities compared to Customer B's. Therefore, the design of Customer A's CO2 recovery plant would need to accommodate this higher impurity level, requiring additional capacity or specific equipment to handle it effectively.

<u>By analyzing the raw CO2 purity and impurities beforehand, the CO2 recovery plant can be designed with precision, ensuring optimal performance and reliability for each customer's unique requirements.</u>

CO2 Plant Process Flow Diagram, Design, and Sizing of Equipment

> *As mentioned in the previous chapter, once the purity and impurities of raw CO2 are known, designing a CO2 recovery plant starts with creating a process flow diagram. This diagram outlines how the plant will operate to produce the desired output of liquid CO2.*

It's important to understand that not all CO2 recovery plants can produce high-purity liquid CO2 suitable for beverage or welding applications. Before finalizing the CO2 recovery plant, identifying your target customers, helps to determine the number and size of equipment needed for the CO2 recovery plant.

During my recent visit to a Distillery located near Kanpur, India, I noticed that the CO2 recovery plant installed there lacked basic equipment like stripper columns or reboilers.

This CO_2 recovery plant struggles to produce high- purity liquid CO_2.

During my visit to another CO_2 recovery plant, I noticed that stripper column and reboiler were installed, but those equipment were not properly sized to purify the liquid CO_2 to the desired purity and impurity levels.

If your target is to produce high-purity liquid CO_2 for beverage or welding applications, specific equipment like stripper columns and reboilers are essential. However, if the target is different, the equipment configuration will vary accordingly.

<u>Therefore, it's crucial to ensure that the CO_2 recovery plant is equipped with the right size and type of equipment to achieve the desired purity levels and meet the requirements of the targeted customers. This ensures efficient operation and consistent quality of the liquid CO_2 output.</u>

Material of Construction of Equipment

Normally, CO2 plant equipment and piping are constructed from a combination of various materials such as SS 304 (or SS 316) OR SA 516 Grade 70 (for piping, SA 333 Grade 6).

When it comes to equipment that comes into contact with wet or moist carbon dioxide, stainless steel grades like SS 304 or SS 316 are commonly used, including piping. It's also crucial to consider the size of the piping to ensure that the gas velocity through the pipeline is calculated according to engineering standards to achieve the best performance of the plant at optimum cost.

For equipment and piping that come into contact with liquid carbon dioxide having low moisture content (less than 20 ppm), low-temperature steel, such as SA516 Grade 70, is suitable for this purpose. Additionally, for low-temperature applications, pipe materials should meet standards like SA 333 Grade 6 to ensure the safe and efficient operation of the plant.

By using the right materials for equipment and piping and ensuring that they are sized correctly, the CO2 recovery plant can operate safely and effectively, minimizing the risk of corrosion and ensuring the quality of the liquid CO2 output. This ensures compliance with industry standards and regulations, contributing to the overall success of the plant.

SICGIL entered into a long-term contract to buy industrial-grade liquid CO2 from a distillery based in Katrenipalle, Andhra Pradesh, India. The CO2 recovery plant was supplied by a Delhi-based fabricator. The distillery people suffered a lot because, within 15 months of the plant starting, the majority of the liquefier tubes started leaking. After investigation by the SICGIL technical team, it was found that the material of construction (MOC) of the liquefier tubes was incorrect. Finally, on the advice of SICGIL, the entire liquefier was replaced with one having SS tubes and a larger size.

Design Standard & Safe Operating Pressure of Plant vs. Design Pressure of Plant

All the equipment must be designed as per ASME Section VIII. Normally, CO2 equipment is designed for a pressure of 27.5 kg/cm^2(g), while the operating pressure for a CO2 plant typically ranges from 17.0 to 21.0 kg/cm^2(g).

Chapter 4

Selection of CO2 Compressor & Selection of Ammonia Compressor

> *Generally, CO2 recovery plant installers use two different types of Compressors for CO2 applications. One is a non-lubricating, three-stage reciprocating compressor and the other is a lubricating screw compressor.*

Non-lubricating type three stage reciprocating compressors are commonly used for CO2 applications. This type of compressor requires maintenance every six months, including the replacement of piston rings, wearing rings, and other regular monitoring maintenance activities. I have observed that some CO2 plants use two-stage compressors instead of three-stage compressors. <u>Two-stage compressors consume 10% more power compared to three-stage compressors.</u>

Another option for a CO2 compressor is an oil-lubricated screw compressor. Normally, screw compressors require major maintenance every 30,000 to 40,000 hours of operation. Monitoring bearing wear and tear is essential to extend the maintenance intervals. If a screw compressor is selected, a special filter must be used to prevent oil particles being carried along with the discharged CO2 gas. *It is crucial to consider that a screw compressor should be a two-stage compressor on a single motor shaft, rather than two separate compressors on a skid.* Two different compressors on a skid may create safety concerns in the event of instrumentation failure.

Similar to CO2 compressors, there are two choices for Ammonia Compressors: One is a two-stage reciprocating oil-lubricated compressor, and the other is a two-stage single-shaft lubricated screw compressor.

Ammonia Compressors and Their Types

Ammonia compressors play a crucial role in various industrial applications, particularly in refrigeration systems. These compressors are designed to handle ammonia as a refrigerant, which is favored for its efficiency, low environmental impact, and cost-effectiveness. There are primarily two types of ammonia compressors: reciprocating compressors and screw compressors.

1. **Reciprocating Compressors:** Reciprocating compressors, also known as piston compressors, operate using a piston-cylinder mechanism. They are widely used in ammonia applications due to their robustness and ability to handle

     Smart Investment in CO_2 Recovery

high-pressure conditions. Reciprocating compressors can be further categorized into two types:

- **Single-Stage Compressors:** These compressors are suitable for lower pressure applications and are typically used in smaller systems.

- **Two-Stage Compressors:** These compressors are designed for higher pressure applications, providing better efficiency and performance. They require maintenance every twelve months, including the replacement of piston rings, wearing rings, and regular monitoring of the oil level.

Advantages of Reciprocating Compressors:

- High efficiency for a wide range of pressure conditions.

- Suitable for intermittent and continuous operations.

- Robust design and long lifespan.

2. **Screw Compressors:** Screw compressors, also known as rotary compressors, use a pair of meshing helical screws to compress the ammonia gas. These compressors are oil-lubricated and are preferred for their continuous operation capabilities and lower maintenance requirements. Screw compressors can also be categorized into:

- **Single-Stage Compressors:** These compressors have single stages of compression on a motor shaft, ensuring better reliability and safety. Power consumption will be higher for this option compared to two-stage compressors on a single shaft. Alternatively, two separate compressors can be used for each stage of compression to save power.

- **Two-Stage Compressors on a Single Shaft:** These compressors offer higher efficiency and reduced safety concerns compared to systems with two different compressors on a skid.

Advantages of Screw Compressors:

- Continuous and smooth operation with less vibration.
- Lower maintenance intervals, typically every 30,000 to 40,000 hours.
- High reliability and efficiency for large-scale applications.

Choosing the Right Compressor

Selecting the appropriate ammonia compressor depends on various factors, including the specific application, pressure requirements, and maintenance capabilities. For high-pressure and high-efficiency needs, two-stage reciprocating compressors or two-stage screw compressors on a single shaft are ideal choices. Regular monitoring and maintenance, such as using online vibration sensors for bearing wear, can enhance the lifespan and performance of these compressors.

Ammonia compressors are essential for efficient and sustainable industrial refrigeration, ensuring optimal performance and adherence to environmental standards.

In Chapter 6, I have explained the benefits of Ammonia as the right choice of refrigerant.

For screw compressors, whether for CO2 or ammonia applications, **The Bearings Can Be Monitored Through An Online Vibration Sensor to Prevent Major Compressor Failures.**

Design and Performance of Water-Cooled Heat Exchanger

> *Electric Power is one of the raw materials for CO2 recovery plants, contributing significantly to operating costs. The right size and design of a water-cooled heat exchanger can minimize power consumption, thereby operating costs.*

In the past, I visited a CO2 recovery plant in Asmoli, UP, and a distillery in Kanpur. A common issue was found in both CO2 recovery plants: the water-cooled heat exchangers for the CO2 compressors were incorrectly designed, with water passing through the shell side and gas through the tube side. As a result, the CO2 gas temperature at the outlet of the heat exchanger exceeded 50-55°C, despite the water inlet temperature being around 30°C. This design flaw reduces the output of the CO2 compressor and consequently, the entire CO2 recovery plant, leading to increased power consumption.

The aforementioned heat exchangers were smaller in size, which provided a cost advantage to the CO2 plant supplier but was disadvantageous for the CO2 recovery plant owner. This temporary advantage of lower capital costs for the heat exchanger is offset by the long-term disadvantage of deteriorating performance. As water passes through the shell side, scaling occurs on the outer surface of the tubes over time. Cleaning the outer surface of all the tubes is difficult, even if the tube bundle is removable. Due to scaling, the delta temperature (CO2 outlet temperature minus water inlet temperature) increases, raising the overall gas outlet temperature from the heat exchanger. This affects the performance of subsequent equipment and reduces compressor efficiency, leading to increased power consumption and operating costs.

<u>For all water-cooled heat exchangers, my recommendation is that water should pass through the tube side and gas through the shell side.</u> This type of design will make the heat exchanger larger in size. In this configuration, the gas is on the shell side. The shell plate thickness should be calculated according to the gas pressure on the shell side, considering safety factors and HAZOP recommendations. With this design, water passes through the tube side, making internal cleaning of the tubes easier. Although this type of heat exchanger (H/X) design increases capital expenditure slightly, the overall operating costs will be lower.

Why Ammonia as a Refrigerant?

> *Ammonia has a higher latent heat of evaporation compared to other refrigerants, requiring less quantity for the same cooling effect. Overall, the heat exchanger size will be much smaller compared to other refrigerants.*

1. **Temperature Requirements:** Ammonia needs to achieve a temperature range of approximately minus 32 to minus 33 degrees Celsius to liquefy the CO2 in the cycle.

2. **Heat Removal:** Heat is removed from the ammonia using evaporative condensers, where the entire tubes are immersed in water to cool the ammonia as close to the wet bulb temperature of water as possible.

3. **Suitability of Ammonia:**
    - Ammonia is chosen for its availability and cost-effectiveness, priced at around less than 1 USD per

kilogram compared to other refrigerants which cost 7-8 USD per kilogram.

- **Ammonia requires smaller line sizes and has a higher coefficient of performance compared to other refrigerants.**

- **Ammonia operates at lower condensation pressure and temperature, resulting in lower power consumption.**

- Its flooded design allows for better efficiency in heat transfer.

4. **Usage of Ammonia in India:** Ammonia has been used as a refrigerant gas for over 40 years.

5. **Superiority over F-gases:** Ammonia proves to be a superior alternative to F-gases, especially with the global ban on HFC gases due to ozone layer depletion.

6. **Managing Toxicity Issues:** Safety measures such as vessel design, safety valves, automation, instrumentation, and online ammonia leak detectors are implemented to ensure process safety.

7. **Maintenance and Top-up:** Ammonia systems typically do not require topping up if there is no leakage. Ammonia purifiers are used to remove air, oil, and water from the system to maintain efficiency.

8. **Identification and Correction of Contamination:** Ammonia purifiers help identify and remove oil and water contamination from the system.

9. **Handling During Maintenance of Equipment in Ammonia Chilling System:** Ammonia is pumped down to the receiver and condenser before maintenance, and the remaining ammonia in the system is removed safely by diluting it with water. After this, maintenance can be carried out. **A key design parameter to consider is the ammonia receiver size, considering the standard filling ratio of liquified ammonia. Additionally, having a correct level measurement system for the ammonia receiver is important. There have been cases of ammonia receivers bursting due to incorrect or smaller sizes.**

10. **Ammonia Grade:** Industrial or commercial grade ammonia with a purity of 99.8% is commonly used. The purity of ammonia in the system can be improved using an ammonia purifier.

11. **Applicability:** Ammonia can be used in most parts of the world, with specific design considerations required for extremely warm climates.

12. **SICGIL, Leader of the CO2 Industry in India:** SICGIL operates more than 25 CO2 liquefiers with ammonia chillers, having ammonia compressors with electric motors ranging from 375 KW to 550 KW for ammonia compression.

13. **Compressor Configuration:** Two-stage compressors with ammonia intercooling are preferred for ammonia compression, offering efficient operation and power

consumption. It's crucial not to overcharge the system with ammonia. Plate-type heat exchangers are used for sub-cooling to enhance plant efficiency.

In conclusion, ammonia stands out as an efficient, cost-effective, and environmentally friendly refrigerant, making it an excellent choice for industrial applications.

7
Chapter

Insulation of Low-Temperature Equipment

> *Proper insulation is essential for all piping and equipment carrying fluids with temperatures lower than 10°C. This insulation helps prevent heat transfer and maintains the desired low temperatures efficiently. Poor insulation results in the loss of cold energy and increased power consumption.*

➤ **Recommended Insulation Method:** In-situ polyurethane foam (PUF) insulation with aluminum cladding is highly recommended for low-temperature equipment. This type of insulation provides excellent thermal resistance and protection against moisture.

➤ **Importance of Insulation Quality:** It's crucial to ensure that the insulation is applied correctly and effectively. Any wet spots or moisture on the exterior of cold pipelines or equipment indicate weak or ineffective insulation. These wet spots lead to heat loss and increase overall power consumption.

> **Preventing Heat Loss:** Efficient insulation prevents cold energy from escaping, thereby reducing the need for additional cooling and lowering energy consumption. By maintaining consistent low temperatures, the insulation also ensures optimal performance and prolongs the lifespan of equipment.

Additional Technical Considerations

> **Insulation Thickness:** The thickness of insulation should be adequate to provide sufficient thermal resistance and prevent heat transfer. A small cost saving by using thinner insulation will lead to much higher operating costs due to additional power consumption.

> **Inspection and Maintenance:** Regular inspection and maintenance of insulation are necessary to identify and address any issues such as damage, wear, or moisture ingress.

> **Environmental Factors:** Consideration should be given to environmental factors such as humidity, temperature variations, and exposure to the elements, which can affect insulation performance.

> **Insulation Material:** While PUF insulation with aluminum cladding is commonly used, other insulation materials such as mineral wool or fiberglass may also be suitable depending on specific requirements and conditions.

By ensuring proper insulation of low-temperature equipment, CO2 plants installed by ethanol manufacturers can optimize energy efficiency, reduce operating costs, and maintain the integrity of their processes.

○ ○ ○ ○

Chapter 8

Easy Installation of SKID Mounted Plants

> *When considering the purchase of a CO2 recovery plant, opting for a skid-mounted plant offers several benefits in terms of installation. Skid-mounted plants provide flexibility in transport and erection, significantly reducing the need for onsite fabrication work and resulting in faster installation.*

➢ **Flexibility and Transport:** Skid-mounted plants provide flexibility in transport and erection, making them easier to move and install at the desired location. The entire plant is pre-mounted on a sturdy steel frame (skid), allowing for simplified transportation to the site.

➢ **Reduced Fabrication Work:** Skid-mounted plants significantly reduce the need for onsite fabrication work, as most components are pre-assembled and tested at the factory. This leads to substantial time savings and streamlines the installation process.

➢ **Faster Installation:** Due to the pre-assembled nature of skid-mounted plants, installation time is significantly reduced. In fact, skid-mounted plants can be installed in as little as 25% of the time required for traditional plants without skids. This expedited installation process minimizes downtime and allows for quicker commissioning of the plant.

➢ **Pre-Tested Interconnections:** Interconnecting piping, valves, and components on skid-mounted plants are thoroughly tested at the factory before being fitted into the skid. As a result, onsite pressure testing of interconnecting piping is minimized or eliminated, saving both time and labor during installation.

➢ **Technical Considerations:**

- **Quality Assurance:** Skid-mounted plants undergo rigorous quality control checks and testing procedures during the manufacturing process to ensure reliability and performance.

- **Customization Options:** Despite being pre-mounted, skid-mounted plants can still offer customization options to suit specific requirements and operational needs.

- **Space Efficiency:** Skid-mounted plants are designed to maximize space efficiency, making them ideal for installations where space is limited or costly.

By choosing a skid-mounted CO2 recovery plant, ethanol manufacturers can benefit from streamlined installation, reduced downtime, and enhanced operational efficiency, ultimately contributing to cost savings and improved productivity.

○　○　○　○

Instrumentation, Automation, Hazop Study of Plant

Instrumentation and automation play a crucial role in ensuring the safe and efficient operation of CO2 recovery plants. Properly implemented instrumentation provides real-time monitoring and control of key process parameters, while automation reduces manual intervention and enhances operational efficiency.

Digital pressure, temperature, and flow transmitters connected with audio-visual alarms make CO2 recovery plants safer. Additionally, Mechanical Safety Valves fitted on pressure vessels, storage tanks, and pipelines ensure that the CO2 plant operates within the specific pressure range.

Key Aspects of Instrumentation

➢ **Process Monitoring:** Instruments such as pressure gauges, pressure transmitters, flow meters, and temperature sensors are installed to continuously monitor process variables.

> **Safety Systems:** Instrumentation includes safety devices such as pressure relief valves, emergency shutdown systems, and gas leak detectors to safeguard against potential hazards.

> **Control Systems:** Automated control systems regulate process conditions to maintain optimal performance and maximize yield while minimizing energy consumption.

Advantages of Automation

> **Enhanced Safety:** Automation reduces the risk of human error and ensures consistent adherence to safety protocols, thereby enhancing overall plant safety.

> **Improved Efficiency:** Automated control systems optimize process parameters in real-time, resulting in higher efficiency, increased productivity, and reduced operating costs.

> **Remote Monitoring and Control:** Automation enables remote monitoring and control of plant operations, allowing for timely adjustments and troubleshooting, even from off-site locations.

Importance of Hazop Study

A Hazop (Hazard and Operability) study is a systematic process hazard analysis method used to identify potential hazards, deviations from design intent, and operability issues in CO2 recovery plants.

> ➤ **Key Components of Hazop Study:**
>
> - **Identification of Hazards:** The Hazop study systematically examines each process parameter and identifies potential hazards, including equipment failures, process deviations, and human errors.
>
> - **Risk Assessment:** The Hazop study assesses the severity and likelihood of identified hazards to prioritize mitigation measures and allocate resources effectively.
>
> - **Recommendations for Safety Measures:** Based on the findings of the Hazop study, recommendations are made for additional safety devices, instrumentation upgrades, and operational procedures to mitigate identified risks.

Continuous Improvement

<u>A Hazop study is not a one-time activity but an ongoing process that should be periodically reviewed and updated to address changes in plant operations, technology advancements, and regulatory requirements.</u>

By emphasizing the importance of instrumentation, automation, and Hazop study, ethanol manufacturers can ensure the safe, efficient, and reliable operation of their CO2 recovery plants, thereby minimizing risks and maximizing productivity.

Chapter 10

Desiccant Bed & Deodorizer Bed

Lacking in the design of the desiccant Bed and Deodorizer Bed, with respect to their size and the selection of the right desiccant, can create major issues for efficient removal of moisture from the incoming gas stream.

The same way, a lack of design in the deodorizer bed with respect to its size & selection of make and grade can create major issues for the efficient removal of certain impurities from the incoming gas stream.

These issues will affect plant yield and mainly product quality.

Method of Regeneration for Desiccant Bed & Deodorizer Bed

Thermal regeneration method involves heating the desiccant beds to a high temperature to drive off the moisture adsorbed during the adsorption cycle. The heat source can be hot air, steam, or electric heating elements.

> **Effect of Regeneration on Plant Yield:**

- **Improved Efficiency:** Proper regeneration of desiccant beds and deodorizer bed ensures that impurities are effectively removed from the incoming gas stream during the adsorption cycle. This results in higher purity and yield of the recovered CO2.

- **Reduced Loss of Pure CO2:** A well-designed desiccant bed and deodorizer bed minimize the loss of pure CO2 from the tank, leading to higher overall yield and improved product quality.

- **Consistent Performance:** Regular regeneration of desiccant beds and deodorizer beds helps maintain consistent performance and prevents the carryover of moisture and other impurities in the system, ensuring reliable operation of the CO2 recovery plant.

> **Optimizing Desiccant Bed Design:**

- **Bed Size and Configuration:** The size and configuration of desiccant bed and deodorizer bed should be optimized to maximize contact between the gas stream and the desiccant material, ensuring efficient impurity absorption and removal.

- **Regeneration Cycle Frequency:** The frequency of regeneration cycles should be carefully determined based on the specific operating conditions and the moisture content as well as the impurity level of the incoming gas stream.

- **Monitoring and Control:** Continuous monitoring of key parameters such as temperature and pressure during the regeneration process is essential for optimal performance and efficiency. It is also necessary to monitor moisture content and specific impurities to be removed through the deodorizer bed at the outlet of the purification bed.

By emphasizing the importance of proper regeneration techniques, ethanol manufacturers can enhance the performance, yield, and reliability of their CO2 recovery plants, ultimately contributing to improved product quality and operational efficiency.

11 Chapter

Periodic Maintenance and Its Effect on Power Consumption

> *Maintaining proper maintenance practices is essential for the efficient and reliable operation of CO2 recovery plants. Neglecting maintenance tasks can lead to increased power consumption and reduced plant performance.*

➢ **Key Maintenance Considerations:**

- **Preventive Maintenance:** Implementing a proactive maintenance schedule is crucial to prevent unexpected breakdowns and ensure continuous operation. Regular inspections, lubrication of moving parts, and replacement of worn components are essential preventive measures.

- **Heat Exchanger Cleaning:** Regular cleaning of heat exchangers is necessary to prevent fouling and scaling, which can impair heat transfer efficiency. Fouling reduces the effectiveness of heat exchange, leading to increased power consumption to maintain desired process temperatures.

- **Process Parameter Monitoring:** Continuous monitoring of process parameters such as temperature, pressure, and flow rates is essential to detect deviations from normal operating conditions. Any abnormalities should be promptly addressed through maintenance and corrective actions to prevent energy wastage.

➤ **Impact on Power Consumption:**

- **Efficiency:** Proper maintenance ensures that equipment operates at optimal efficiency, reducing energy losses and minimizing power consumption.

- **Process Stability:** Regular maintenance helps maintain process stability, preventing fluctuations in operating conditions that can lead to increased energy requirements.

- **Long-Term Cost Savings:** Investing in preventive maintenance reduces the risk of costly repairs and downtime, ultimately resulting in long-term cost savings through improved energy efficiency and operational reliability.

➤ **Continuous Improvement:**

- **Training and Education:** Providing comprehensive training to plant operators and maintenance staff ensures they understand the importance of maintenance practices and are equipped to perform their roles effectively.

- **Data Analysis:** Utilizing data analytics and condition monitoring techniques can help identify maintenance needs proactively, allowing for timely interventions to optimize plant performance and minimize energy consumption.

- **Benchmarking:** Comparing energy consumption data against industry benchmarks and best practices can highlight areas for improvement and guide efforts to further enhance energy efficiency.

By prioritizing preventive maintenance and adopting strategies to optimize energy consumption, ethanol manufacturers can ensure the reliable operation and sustainable performance of their CO2 recovery plants, contributing to operational excellence and cost-effectiveness.

As an industry standard, every ton of Liquid Co2 produced through a recovery plant should not exceed a specific power consumption of 200 kW per ton. Specific power consumption will increase if the raw CO2 purity is less than 99.8 %, or if the plant equipment and process flow are poorly designed. These factors play a significant role in the power consumption of Liquid CO2 production.

Chapter 12

Training For Plant Operators & Engineers

> *Operating a CO2 recovery plant requires specialized knowledge and skills due to the potentially hazardous nature of the process. Proper training is essential to ensure the safety of personnel and the efficient operation of the plant.*

Ensure that your CO2 recovery plant supplier is capable and provide sufficient training to operate and maintain the plant. Periodic training as part of after-sales service is also a crucial component to consider when purchasing a CO2 recovery plant.

Additionally, your CO2 recovery plant supplier should conduct periodic audits once the plant has been installed, including:

➤ Identifying potential unsafe conditions

- Validating the competency of Plant Operators & Engineers

- Training Plant Operators & Engineers and checking its effectiveness

- Performing health checks on plant equipment and reviewing maintenance activities

Key Training Components

- **Safety Protocols:** Plant operators and engineers must receive comprehensive training on safety protocols and Standard Operating Procedures to mitigate risks associated with handling CO_2 and other hazardous materials. This includes understanding the properties of CO_2, recognizing potential hazards, and knowing how to respond to emergencies.

- **Operating Procedures:** Training should cover the operating procedures specific to the CO_2 recovery plant, including start-up and shutdown sequences, equipment operation, and troubleshooting techniques. Operators should be familiar with all aspects of plant operation to ensure smooth and efficient performance.

- **Maintenance Practices:** Operators and engineers should be trained in preventive maintenance practices to ensure the ongoing reliability and performance of the plant. This includes routine inspections, lubrication schedules, and equipment troubleshooting.

> **Emergency Response:** Training should include emergency response procedures for handling leaks, spills, and other hazardous situations. Operators must know how to use personal protective equipment (PPE) and emergency response tools, as well as how to evacuate the area safely if necessary.

Displaying Do's and Don'ts

> **Clear Communication:** Displaying clear instructions and guidelines in the plant area ensures that operators are aware of best practices and safety precautions. This includes instructions on handling CO_2, ammonia, and other hazardous materials, as well as emergency contact information.

> **Emergency Procedures:** Do's and don'ts should include specific instructions for responding to common emergencies, such as leaks or spills. Operators should know when to evacuate the area, how to control the hazard, and who to contact for assistance.

Handling Hazardous Situations

> **Ammonia or Carbon Dioxide Leaks:** In the event of a leak, operators must be capable of responding quickly and effectively while wearing appropriate PPE, such as self-contained breathing apparatus (SCBA). Training should emphasize the importance of swift action to minimize risks to personnel and the environment.

> **Safety Equipment:** Operators should be familiar with the location and use of safety equipment, including emergency showers, eyewash stations, and first aid kits. Regular drills and simulations can help reinforce proper response procedures and ensure readiness in case of an emergency.

By providing comprehensive training to plant operators and engineers, ethanol manufacturers can foster a culture of safety and proficiency, minimizing risks and maximizing the efficiency and reliability of their CO2 recovery plants.

Fuel The Future

Congratulations on finishing this insightful exploration! Now, imagine taking your ethanol production to a whole new level of sustainability. With a strategically implemented CO2 recovery plant, you can:

➤ Slash Your Carbon Footprint

➤ Boost Profitability

➤ Future-Proof Your Business

But how do you navigate the complexities of CO2 recovery plant installation?

That's where I come in. I'm here to offer you **exclusive, personalized guidance** tailored to your specific CO2 recovery plant setup at your ethanol manufacturing plant.

➤ **Here's what you'll gain by reaching out:**

- **Expert consultation:** Discuss your unique needs and goals with a CO2 recovery specialist.

- **In-depth analysis:** We'll assess your plant's suitability for CO2 capture and identify the optimal recovery solution.

- **Tailored implementation plan:** Get a road map for a smooth and efficient installation process.

Don't miss this opportunity to unlock the green potential of your ethanol plant.

Pulin Modi CO2 Recovery Specialist, SICGIL

Email: *pulinmodi@sicgil.com*

❍ ❍ ❍ ❍